FINDIN

Anne Fothergill

Front cover picture: The Tower at Stobhill Hospital, Glasgow.

ISBN: 978-1-907257-85-8

Published in 2015 by

Quoin Publishing Ltd.

Other books by the author

It is January 1951. Two-year-old Anne Traynor's world is about to change forever when her mother walks out on her family. She leaves behind her husband, Raphy, son Denis and daughters Elizabeth and Anne.

Ten days later Elizabeth and Anne are taken to a convent in Middlesbrough run by the poor sisters of Nazareth.

Nazareth House, where the rules are strict and there is the ever-present threat from the bullies, the nuns and, according to them, even from God.

Friendships are formed and there is camaraderie among the girls – and rules are there to be broken.

A humorous and illuminating account of Anne's thirteen years spent in care.

'Well written and very absorbing as an account of an important aspect of recent social history written out of first-hand experience' – Jo Heather (Mudfog Press).

It is 1966 and 17-year-old Anne Traynor has left Nazareth House, the orphanage where she spent thirteen years of her life.

Now free from the restrictions imposed on her by the nuns, she is able to make her own way in the world. With the impetuosity of youth Anne, along with her new found friend Katie, they decide to leave the north- east and head for the bright lights of Manchester.

They board a train from Middlesbrough railway station with only a packet of crisps, a carton of milk and very little money.

On arrival in Manchester they look for cheap accommodation to rent. The only suitable digs they can find is a bedsit in Cheetham Hill. It is owned by Jewish landlady Mrs Lowe who says she runs a 'respectable house' and 'no riffraff's allowed'. But all is not what it seems. Why do its tenants call it the Den of Iniquity?

Naive and innocent Anne is plummeted into a colourful world, which is completely at odds with her strict Catholic upbringing and will change her forever.

Background

In June 1976 my mother died. My sister Elizabeth came to my house to inform me. At the time Alan, my husband, and I were living on a council estate in Stockton on Tees with our two young sons. It was not a total surprise as Mother had been diagnosed with cancer a few months earlier. I think she knew that it was terminal. She had rung me up on the telephone to tell me she'd had a big operation. Now she had died. I felt bereft. Even though she had not been our mother in the true sense of the word she had given me life and besides, our relationship was changing for the better. She had met Alan and was getting to know her grandchildren. I suppose that I felt robbed. All those wasted years and now she was gone, just when she had come back into our lives.

Elizabeth knew where Raphy, her dad, was living in Middlesbrough and as he was still married to our mother she thought it only right to tell him. When she went round to see him he took the news well. There was no love lost between him and Mother. They had been living apart for nearly twenty five years.

"Well then," he said to Elizabeth, "you might as well have a look at these two letters that I have had in my possession since 1951."

The letters were from the registrar at Stobhill Hospital in Glasgow asking him if he knew the whereabouts of his wife. Apparently Mother had given birth to a baby on the 25th of

Elizabeth, me and Dennis, 1950.

May 1951 and had walked out of the hospital and nobody knew where she was living. Raphy said he knew that he was not the father and did not know where Mother was and quite simply did not want to get involved so he did not reply. A few weeks later he received another letter from the registrar which said, "I understand that you are not the father of this child but do you have any idea where your wife is?" Again, Raphy did not reply. He told Elizabeth that he did not want to get Mother into trouble.

Elizabeth read the letter. She was shocked to learn that we had a younger sibling and did not know if it was a boy or a girl. When she told me I was equally shocked but then it made sense as to why Mother had just walked out and left her husband and three children on that cold January morning in 1951. Ten days later Raphy had taken Elizabeth and I to Nazareth House in Middlesbrough - an orphanage run by nuns - and simply reneged his responsibility to us. It would be many years before we would see him again. So now we learned that we had a younger brother or sister but where was this sibling of ours? We had to find out. We were soon to face our first setback when we discovered that the maternity unit in Stobhill Hospital had been demolished and all the records had been transferred. We needed a birth certificate. Elizabeth wrote to the General Registrar of Births and Deaths in Edinburgh but they could not help. It was difficult, anyway, as we did not have a name for the baby or even know its gender. Was it still alive? Elizabeth and I thought about the differing scenarios that could have happened. Obviously our mother had not kept the baby so we came to the conclusion that it must have been adopted. Whether it was a private adoption or not we could only guess.

Elizabeth and I attended Mother's funeral in Liverpool. Apart from Jimmy (Mother's partner) and the vicar there were no other mourners. It was so sad.

In 1977 our family suffered another bereavement when our brother Denis was tragically killed at the age of thirty nine. It made me think at the time that if we did find our sibling they would never get the chance to meet their mother or brother. It was a traumatic time for Elizabeth and I, losing Denis when we had just made contact with him again after many years apart. Both he and Mother had not spoken to each other for years so there was no reconciliation between them before she died.

Elizabeth had got in touch with him again through Raphy. Denis wrote me a letter. It came out of the blue. I remember the joy I felt on receiving it. He had written about his wife and step-children and also about his concerns for the future. Little did I know that the letter would be his last. It's a precious memento which I treasure to this day. He also spoke to my two boys on the telephone, although he did most of the talking as the boys were shy and not used to speaking on the phone. Elizabeth had been through to the Midlands where he was living and met his wife and step-daughter. Denis had planned to visit us and meet our children but he never got the chance. Elizabeth and I attended his funeral. I was numb with shock and I was also recovering from a miscarriage.

Then, in 1978, Raphy died. He had been suffering from lung cancer and passed away aged seventy-eight. The 1970s were a mixture of heartache and joy for me; losing Mother, Denis and Raphy but also giving birth to my three children, the youngest a daughter in 1979.

Elizabeth and I got on with raising our own families, but the baby was never far from our thoughts, especially so on the 25th of May, its birthday. The years went by and in 2004 my niece Marie, Elizabeth's daughter, decided to try and help find this relation of ours. She'd heard of the agency Birthlink which was based in Edinburgh and she contacted them giving details about the baby. She received a reply and was informed that we could purchase a record of the birth for ten pounds. It was fantastic news. A week later she received a copy of a birth certificate for an Eileen Mary Waldie Traynor who was born on the 25th of May in 1951 in Glasgow. On the top of the certificate written in ink was the word 'adopted'. We were delighted. We did indeed have a younger sibling and it was a girl. And I was not the baby of the family after all. Elizabeth and I were more determined than ever to look for her.

However, there were more setbacks. First we were to find out that as siblings we had no right to know the details of her adoption. It was up to the adoptee to contact the adoption agency herself. This was frustrating for us. What if she did not know that she had been adopted? Her adoptive parents would no doubt have changed her surname, but would they have kept her Christian name? Had Eileen already found out who her natural birth mother was? Had she already accessed the details of her adoption and not wanted to take it further? Had she married and changed her name?

"Surely she would have needed to show her original birth certificate?" I asked the lady at the agency.

"Not necessarily," she replied. "She would have been given a new birth certificate when she had been adopted. The new birth certificate would have stated that she was the daughter of her adopted parents."

How then could she connect to us, her siblings, who had been born and brought up in England? Who could she contact in Scotland? We had no relatives living there. There were so many unanswered questions and we seemed to be hitting one brick wall after another.

Elizabeth and I contacted the various adoption agencies in both England and Scotland and left our details in case Eileen was to get in touch with any of them. And although it was frustrating all we could do was just wait for a response. More years went by - there were no researchers from the Long Lost Family series to help us. In 2004, with renewed effort, Elizabeth and a friend decided to go to Glasgow and then on to Edinburgh to glean any information about Eileen they could. In Glasgow they went into the Mitchell Library and searched via microfiche old newspaper files for any reference to a mother abandoning her baby in 1951. There was none.

While she was in Stobhill Hospital in 1951 our mother had given her usual address as 133, Ryeside Road, Glasgow. That address was written on the record of the birth certificate that we had received from Birthlink. Elizabeth explained the situation to the librarian who proved to be very helpful and she suggested that she look on the electoral roll to see who was living at that address in 1951. The name that came up was 'Jordan' and again on an up to date electoral roll entry which gave us hope the same person was still living there. Elizabeth decided to go to the house but was disappointed to find that there was nobody at home. She did not want to leave any information with the neighbours, thus she had no choice but to leave.

In Edinburgh, Elizabeth went to the Register Office but because Eileen had been adopted she was not allowed to access the file. Elizabeth was disappointed as she had to return home and felt that we were no further forward. But a few days later she received a letter from the librarian who gave her the phone number of the house in Ryeside Road. Elizabeth eagerly rang the number. A woman answered and said that she had lived in the house all her life and that it had belonged to her mother, a Mrs. Mary Jordan who was now deceased. The woman informed her that she had not heard of our mother and certainly knew nothing about any baby. It was another setback.

In 2010 a friend told Elizabeth about a website that had been set up to help Scots people trace long lost relatives living at home or abroad. On the 25th of May 2010, which would be Eileen's 59th birthday, Elizabeth posted a request on the site asking for details about our sister. In September, she received a reply.

CHAPTER 1

We've found her

The phone rang. I answered it with a casual 'hello'.

"Are you sitting down?" the voice at the other end of the line asked. It was my sister Elizabeth calling.

"I've found Eileen," she said.

"What!" I nearly dropped the phone. "You have found her at last?"

"I've just been talking to her."

"How did she get in touch with you?"

"Remember the message I put on that Lookup UK site on the internet?"

I did. We had exhausted every avenue looking for her in the UK and as a last resort a friend had suggested that we put her details on the message board of this site. Apparently it had been set up so that people that had been brought up abroad could trace their long lost relatives.

Elizabeth and I were now in our sixties and Eileen would soon be reaching her sixtieth birthday. It would be our last hope of finding her. The message had been posted on what would have been Eileen's fifty ninth birthday. It read:

Elizabeth Traynor   Middlesbrough   May 25 2010
I am looking for my sister who was born in Stobhill
Hospital in Glasgow Scotland on 25 May 1951. She was
adopted privately and her name at birth was Eileen Mary
Waldie Traynor. Obviously I do not know her adopted name,

1

although I have traced the birth entry in the Registry Office at Edinburgh, if anyone has any information regarding Eileen please contact me on the above e-mail address.

In September 2010, Eileen had googled her name and that site had come up. It seemed we had struck gold.

"She said that it was such a shock when she saw her real name," Elizabeth said. "She had googled Eileen Mary Waldie Traynor many times before but without success. Then just by chance she had tried again and had been directed to the Lookup UK site. She was elated.

"Her adopted parents emigrated to Australia from Edinburgh when she was four years old."

"No wonder we couldn't find her!" I replied.

"She has an Aussie accent. I think she's been well brought up, she sounds posh."

"Not like us then!"

"She's looking forward to talking to you. I've given her your phone number. I told her that I would ring you beforehand to let you know rather than her ringing you out of the blue."

"I'm glad you did, I'd have had a heart attack. She won't know anything about our family medical history, I wonder if she has had any problems?"

"She has e-mailed me some photos of herself. I'll forward them onto you."

"What does she look like?" I asked.

Eileen's baptismal certificate

"She's a six foot, blue eyed blonde."

"Six foot! You're kidding."

"I was surprised when I found out. I know our mam was tall but she wasn't a six footer."

"Maybe she's taken after grandfather George Waldie. He was over six foot and so were his brothers."

"She may have taken after her father, whoever he was."

"Does Eileen look anything like us?"

"It's hard to say. One of the photos was taken at her retirement do. She's certainly tall and slim."

"Nothing like us then. I'm only five foot five, and you're smaller than me. And we're far from size zero. Are you sure that we have the right person?"

"Yes I'm positive. I'll tell you why. That was our Marie's e- mail address that I left on the message board. Eileen e-mailed her back. The e-mail said, I believe that I am Eileen, the person you are looking for.

"Marie asked her if she had any proof as she didn't want to get our hopes up."

"That was thoughtful of her."

3

"Eileen e-mailed her a copy of her baptismal certificate."

"Now that is something we have never seen. I'd never have thought to look for that. What does it say on the baptismal certificate?"

"It showed that Eileen Mary Waldie had been baptised in Saint Philomena's Church in Glasgow in September 1951."

"Oh wow! This is definite proof. Does she have her original birth certificate?"

"No, that's all she had. She said that she found papers relating to her adoption in a chest of drawers when she was younger. And that's how she'd found out that she was adopted."

"How awful, did her adopted parents not tell her?"

"No, and when she asked them they were reluctant to give her any information. She thinks that they did not know anyway. Eileen said that she always knew that they were not her blood relatives. They were dark haired and small and besides being tall and fair, she looks nothing like them."

"Are her adopted parents still alive?'

"No, they're both dead. She asked me if our mother was still alive. I told her that she'd died of cancer in 1976. She imagines our mother to have been even tempered like herself. Apparently her adopted mother had quite a temper on her."

"It's a shame that we will have to shatter the illusion."

"I couldn't tell her about our mother. She'll soon find out when we tell her the whole story. She asked me if there were any more siblings besides you and me."

"Did you tell her about Denis?"

"I told her that we did have an older brother but he had died. I didn't tell her about the circumstances of his death - that would have been too much for her to take in."

"Did she ask how he had died?"

"Yes, I said he'd died in 1977 a year after our mother. I told her that I would explain later. It was an awkward moment, I can tell you."

"It's a pity that we have to tell her at all. It was traumatic enough having to tell our own bairns."

"She didn't know that we had been brought up in a children's home. She actually thought that our mam would have been a teenage unmarried mother when she had given birth to her. She always thought that she would be the oldest of any siblings. She was really surprised to be told that she is the baby in our family."

"Some baby, at six foot tall she could have been a model. And she towers above us, her older sisters. I'm so looking forward to speaking to her. I can't believe that we have found her.

"I'm going to log on and look at those photos you have e-mailed me."

"What will you say to her when she rings you?"

"Something I've wanted to say to her since we found out about her thirty four years ago - a thousand welcomes, little sis, we have found you at last."

Elizabeth had emailed me a few photographs of Eileen showing her at various ages. She also sent me the email that she had received from her. It read:

Hi Elizabeth,

It is so lovely to hear from you. I have just sent some pictures of me to Marie as well as a baptismal form.

I would love to call you – as I live in Australia, please give me the codes for international etc.

I am so pleased to hear from you.

I attach the pictures and the baptismal form so you can see.

Love

Eileen.

Elizabeth had replied:

Hi Eileen,

I can't believe that we have found you at last. My sister and I were only told about you in 1976.

We have tried so hard to find you even travelling to Glasgow to search the files and to look in the Registry Office in Edinburgh.

When your birthday came round again this year I decided to try again and it looks like I was successful this time.

I would really like you to get in touch with me.

If you would like to find out more about your adoption you can write to Birth link, 21 Castle Street Edinburgh, EH2 3DN

Tel 0131 225 6441

They will give you the information they could not provide us with.

Love

Your sister Elizabeth.

The emails flowed back and forth between them. It was such an exciting time.

CHAPTER **2**
Hello little sis

The phone rang. I picked it up with a mixture of excitement and trepidation.

"Hello," I said.

"Hi, this is Eileen," the voice at the other end of the line replied in a relaxed Australian drawl.

"Hello, little sis. I cannot believe that we have found you after all these years."

"I am so thrilled that I have found my birth family," she told me. "Many times over the years I would go on the internet and google the name that was on the baptismal certificate but nothing ever came up."

"I would do the same myself when we were looking for you."

"I have had a lovely chat to Elizabeth and she told me that you both had been looking for me for years, how wonderful."

"Yes, it was a lucky day when Elizabeth put the message on that web site.

"We often wondered why Mother had given you the name Eileen. Elizabeth is named after Raphy's sister who died before she was born. I was named after Saint Anne. Were you brought up a Catholic?"

"Oh yes, I went to a Catholic school which was run by nuns."

"Were they nice?"

"Oh yes, most of them were. My mother would have had something to say about it if they had picked on me. Elizabeth told me a little bit about your upbringing in Nazareth House. I was surprised when she said that you had both been brought up in a children's home. It must have been awful for you."

"It's a long story, pet. We have a lot to tell you."

"When I found out that I was adopted I would daydream about my mother. When I found out what my real name was I would look in the mirror and say, 'You are Eileen Mary Waldie Traynor.' It sounded wonderful."

"Mother gave you the option to trace her if you wished - that is what I think because she gave you her names. Her maiden name was Mary Waldie and her married name was Mary Traynor."

"I am thrilled to hear that. I imagined that I would be like her in temperament. I'm quite laid back and I try not to let things faze me. My adopted mother had quite a temper on her. What was our mother like?"

"Ah, well ...", I said, as I struggled to find the words.

I thought of the tale that our mother had told Elizabeth and me. One evening her partner Hugh had arrived home late after a drinking session with his colleagues. He had brought home a fish supper. Our mother was so angry that she'd flung the fish supper back at him, but he had ducked and it had landed on the wall behind him, leaving the grease dripping down the wallpaper.

Our mother was not averse to throwing things about. She had one hell of a temper too.

9

Mother in Liverpool circa 1960.

Better not tell her of the time Mother had chased me up the stairs brandishing an umbrella in a fit of rage.

I tried not to shatter the illusion too much at this stage.

"Well, our mother was a redhead, and you know what they say, that they can be quite fiery."

10

"I read your e-mail and those photos of your family, three children, how wonderful."

"Alan's a Maths teacher and I've been married nearly forty years. I got lucky."

"How lovely."

"You don't have any children?"

"No, I never married. I was engaged once. He was killed in a motoring accident." Her voice tailed off. I detected a sadness there and didn't pursue it.

"I'm sorry we haven't many photos of Mother. That one that Elizabeth e-mailed you was taken when Mother was living in Liverpool. It's not a very good snap-shot."

Mother is sat on a wall, outside a large Georgian house. She is posing for the camera. Her legs are crossed and the tips of the fingers of both hands are placed delicately on the wall on either side of her. Her head is tilted slightly to the left and she is looking away from the camera. There is only a side view of her face.

"Was that Mother's house in the background?"

"I'm not sure, she moved around a lot."

It was nothing like the dingy terraced house where Elizabeth and I would stay with our mother when we visited her in Liverpool.

"How did you find out you were adopted?"

"I found some papers relating to my adoption when I was about ten years of age. They were in a chest of drawers."

"That must have come as a shock to you."

"Not really, I always thought that I was different from them. I remember once when we were in a supermarket and the lady at the till looked at my brother and remarked how like his mother he was. She couldn't say the same about me. Joseph is their own child - my adopted mother could not have any more children after she had him."

"When you found those papers did you ask your parents about them?"

"Yes, but they were reluctant to give me any information. I don't think that they knew much about my real mother. They thought that she may have been an English teacher."

"An English teacher? Whatever gave them that idea? She wasn't English and she wasn't a teacher," I laughed. "And do you know you look just like her?"

"It is lovely to hear that. In all my years growing up in Australia, I would think there is nobody in this country who shares my genes."

"You must have felt quite isolated."

"Yes, at times I did."

"Did you see any resemblance to yourself in the photographs to any members of our family?"

"Certainly, that photo of grandfather George. I look like him."

"He was over six foot and a redhead, and according to Mother had a temper to match. He was the youngest of seven children."

"Did you ever meet him?"

"Just the once.

Grandfather, George Waldie

"Only the once?"

"Yes, he never once came to visit us in Nazareth House. Mother said that he didn't care about us. He and Mother had a tempestuous relationship, they were too much alike. He did not approve of Mother's marriage as Raphy was a Catholic and Grandfather was a staunch Protestant. But he could not have stopped mother getting married to Raphy she would probably have run away with him. I think she was pregnant with Denis at the time."

"Did mother and Grandfather reconcile before he died?"

"No, they didn't. They were both stubborn and proud. It's a Waldie trait me thinks, pet."

"That is so sad."

"Grandfather left her out of his will but under Scottish law Mother was entitled to claim something and she did. She didn't get much though, she said."

"How did you get in touch with Grandfather?"

"Denis gave Elizabeth his address and told her to go and visit him if she wished and we did. I was sixteen when I saw him for the first time. He looked so much like our mother that we knew who he was before we introduced ourselves. He seemed genuinely pleased to see us. I remember he had very light blue eyes and there were tears in them. I asked him why mother had left us in a children's home."

"What did he say?"

"He didn't answer. I told him that we thought Mother had been spoiled and had too much of everything when she was growing up. Looking back, I hope he didn't think that we were blaming him for mother being irresponsible.

"We spent a few hours with Grandfather and when we were leaving he told Elizabeth and I that we were welcome to come and visit him again and that he would pay our fare from England. He loved us, he said, even if we were Catholics. We assured him that we'd had no choice in the matter, but we thought it was a strange thing to say.

"We never saw him again. He died the following year."

"How old was he? Where was he living?"

He was nearly 90, and living in residential care in Hawick in Scotland."

"Wow! That was a good innings, have we got longevity in the family?"

"Well, I don't know about the women. Grandfather outlived four wives. I've traced the family history and the women seem to pop off at the age of sixty four, and that included our mother. Elizabeth and I are in our early sixties now, we're getting worried."

"I was sad to hear that Mother had died. I will never get the chance to meet her. But I am so pleased that I have made contact with my lovely sisters."

CHAPTER 3
Newcastle Airport

I got into the front passenger seat of our car and fastened my seat belt.

My husband slid into the driver's seat.

"Well, you will soon be meeting your adopted sister, how do you feel?" he asked as he started up the engine.

"I'm excited."

"She's a stranger to you."

"I know she is, but I feel that I've got to know her through our e-mails and phone calls."

"But it's different now, you are seeing her in the flesh. Do you think that you will recognise her?"

"Of course I will, she looks just like our mam."

Just then, my mobile rang.

"Hi Elizabeth," I answered. "We're on our way to your place, we'll be there in ten minutes to pick you up. Then we'll head for Newcastle Airport. How are you?"

"I'm tired, didn't get much sleep thinking about meeting Eileen. What about you?"

"I slept like a log, but you know me, it's the medication, it knocks me out."

"Lucky you."

"See you soon."

We arrived at Elizabeth's house.

"Have you stocked up on plenty of veggie stuff?" she asked as she climbed into the back seat of our car. "Eileen's a vegetarian."

"I know, she told me. I've got plenty of fruit and salads."

"I wonder why she's a veggie. Do you think she was brought up as one?"

"No, she only decided a few years ago."

"We won't be having our Sunday roast, pet," I said jokingly to my husband as we drove out of Elizabeth's driveway.

"What! I'm not going without my roast beef. Eileen might just want the veg."

"We can't just give her the veg. And what about the gravy? Can't give her any of that."

"What will you give her then?"

"I can make an alternative meal for her. She is okay with fish and she likes salmon. It's not as if she's a vegan."

"I couldn't be a vegetarian, I like my bacon sarnies," Elizabeth said. "Eileen says she still gets tempted if she gets a whiff of bacon."

"Ah, we will have her eating meat again by the time she gets back to Australia," Alan remarked, before nearly missing our turnoff. He was forced to swerve to get us onto the slip road.

"You concentrate on the driving," I told him as we headed for the A19. "We don't want to get lost and miss her flight arrival."

Angel of The North

"Oh no, that would be awful," Elizabeth replied, "if she arrived at the airport and there was no-one to meet her."

Eileen would be staying with Alan and I for three days, then we had planned for her to stay with Elizabeth before we all took a trip to Scotland.

"Are you worried in case you don't get on? After all, you don't know her," asked Alan.

"Stop being so negative. After all, she is my sister."

"Well, she will be staying in our home. It's okay for me, I'll be at work, but you will have her all day."

"Anne will be fine, she gets on with everybody," my sister laughed. "She's sunny natured."

"Don't get me wrong," Alan said. "I'm looking forward to meeting her. I've spoken to her on the phone and she sounds really nice."

"Of course. Anyone related to me and Elizabeth is bound to be."

"Your mother wasn't."

"Well, nearly everyone," Elizabeth said. "We'll have to be prepared for her asking lots of questions about the family."

"She told me that she is not that interested in knowing who her father was. It's Mother she wants to know about," I said. "It's just as well, because we don't know who he is, either."

"She knows that we were brought up by the nuns in Nazareth House," Elizabeth said. "I told her that Raphy put us in there in January 1951, ten days after Mother walked out on us. I was four and you were only two years old. She was shocked."

"Yes, Elizabeth, I spent thirteen years in that place and you were there even longer."

"Your mother was pregnant with Eileen at the time," Alan said. "That's why she walked out. Do you think that Raphy knew?"

"Apparently not," Elizabeth said. "The first he knew about it was when he got a letter from the registrar asking if he was the father of the baby that she had left at the hospital."

"I find it hard to believe that Raphy didn't know that your mother was five months pregnant when she walked out. She must have been showing."

Elizabeth shrugged her shoulders. "He told me that he didn't know. Another thing - we can't tell Eileen that our mother abandoned her, even if it is true."

"I wonder if Mother had some kind of breakdown after the birth?" I asked. After all, I'd suffered from post-natal depression after the birth of my youngest.

"No way, she was just a selfish bitch," Alan said.

"You men don't understand. Your hormones are all over the place after giving birth."

"I told her that Mother flitted in and out of our lives," Elizabeth said. "We don't really know much about her ourselves, but at least we got to meet our mam. Eileen will never get that chance."

There was silence in the car as we headed onto the A1.

"I think Eileen will have an inkling of what our mother was really like from what we have told her," I said.

"We are coming up to the Angel of the North," Alan said.

I fumbled in my handbag for my mobile.

"Slow down, I've got to get a photo for the grandbairns."

"I can't. There's a car up my backside."

Too late! We'd gone past it.

I looked out of the side window just in time to see the dark outline of the Angel of the North, arms open wide in a welcoming gesture.

Soon we would be welcoming our sister back into the arms of the family she never knew she had.

CHAPTER 4
Eileen Arrives

We pulled into the car park, just as a large Easyjet plane was coming into land.

"Wow! Look at that," I exclaimed, but my stomach was churning. Airports always have that effect on me. I usually have to brace myself when we are about to fly away on holiday.

"Well, she won't be on that one. It's probably coming from Tenerife," Alan said. "Wish I was on it and heading the other way."

"What! You and Anne have just come back from a month in the sun. Haven't you had enough?"

"You can never get enough of the good stuff, Elizabeth. If I could afford it I would live out there."

We got out of the car. "Elizabeth and I will go on ahead while you get a parking ticket," I said.

The airport was unusually quiet. It's normally bustling with passengers but only a few people were mulling about.

I scanned the information board for the international flight arrivals.

"The flight from Melbourne will be arriving in half an hour, Elizabeth It's as well we set off from home when we did."

Alan joined us after parking the car. He was annoyed. "It's scandalous, the car parking fees."

I looked around. "The flight's due in half an hour, maybe we should sit down."

"There are no seats," Alan said, "unless you sit in the café, and the cost of a cuppa in here is daylight robbery. No, we'll wait until Eileen arrives - she'll probably be glad of one after the long flight."

A muffled announcement came over the intercom - something about a flight being delayed.

"Hope it's not Eileen's flight," Alan said. "That's all we need, to be hanging around here. I'll go and check."

"Alan's concerned, isn't he?" Elizabeth remarked.

"He'll be thinking of the car parking fees," I said.

Elizabeth and I watched with bated breath as he looked at the information board. He eventually gave a thumbs up. We breathed a sigh of relief.

Alan rejoined us. "Do you like flying, Elizabeth?"

"Not really."

"Anne used to be terrified of flying. We couldn't go anywhere sunny."

"I know. I was in my fifties before I took my first flight. The thought of going up in an aeroplane would bring me out in a cold sweat. The excuses I would give Alan as to why we couldn't go abroad. It didn't matter when the kids were growing up, we couldn't afford a holiday abroad. But when Alan got into teaching he would moan about being stuck at home in the six weeks holidays and the lousy weather.

"I kept saying I couldn't leave Tessa, our little staffie. But, when she died, I ran out of excuses."

"Do you know, Elizabeth, Anne was so nervous on that first flight to Crete that she actually asked the pilot how long had he been flying? She was worried that he hadn't enough experience."

"Eh, you never, did you Anne?"

"Yes, I did. I laugh about it now, but he looked as if he was just out of nappies. He looked too young to be flying real planes."

"That's not all. When we got on the aeroplane, she asked the stewardess to let her off at the next stop."

"I was only kidding, but those Cretans didn't understand the Brits' humour. She kept an eye on me all through the flight. I bet she thought, 'We have a right troublemaker here.' But nothing could be further from the truth. I didn't dare move. I wouldn't even go to the loo."

"And it was a four hour flight," Alan said.

"It's tiny in there and I'm a big girl. I would have been worried about pulling the chain an' all. The ground might have opened up and I would have fallen through."

"It doesn't bother you so much now, though," Alan said. "We've been flying for over ten years now."

"I can just about tolerate it now," I said.

Elizabeth was anxious. "I hope we get on with Eileen. She will be staying over here for three weeks. I hope she's not disappointed with us. I mean, we are not well off."

"That won't bother her. She will be just delighted to see us, I'm sure."

"Don't tell her that she was abandoned. It might really upset her."

"How do we explain the letter that was sent to Raphy asking if he knew the whereabouts of our mother? If it wasn't for that letter we'd have known nothing about her."

The voice over the intercom announced the arrival of the flight from Melbourne.

I was excited. "Ooh, we'll be seeing her soon."

The passengers from the flight came through the international arrivals. People were embracing each other and there were whoops of delight as they caught sight of loved ones.

We eagerly scanned the women but there was no-one that looked remotely like our sister.

The last of the passengers from the flight walked through the arrivals. There was no sign of Eileen.

"Where is she?" Elizabeth asked anxiously. We were getting concerned. "We can't have missed her?"

We looked back at the last of the passengers. They were already leaving the airport.

"Surely, she can't have gone past us?" Alan asked. Panic gripped us all.

"That was her flight, wasn't it?"

We looked up at the information board and then it dawned on me.

"Oh my God. We are waiting at the wrong stand. We're thinking that she is arriving direct from Melbourne, but did she not say that she would be arriving at Heathrow in the early hours of this morning? She has booked into a hotel at the airport to have a nap and freshen up before taking a flight from Heathrow to Newcastle."

"Oh no," Elizabeth cried. "All this time we've been waiting at the wrong place."

I ran down the corridor as fast as my creaky knees would allow. Elizabeth followed trying to keep up. Alan claimed he needed the loo and disappeared into the gents.

We arrived at the UK flight arrivals. I checked the information board. Eileen's plane had landed ten minutes ago.

"Hope we haven't missed her," I panted. Elizabeth and I had a moment to catch our breaths before passengers started coming through the arrivals. We watched intently, scanning every woman. And then we saw her - tall, blonde and elegant, and wearing a smart camel coat.

"Oh my God," Elizabeth and I said almost in unison. "She is the spitting image of our mam."

We waved to her and she came towards us, smiling warmly.

"Hi, I'm Eileen," she said unassumingly.

Elizabeth embraced her. "Lovely to meet you."

I gave her a hug. "Hello, little sis."

I introduced her to Alan. I was glad that at six foot two he was taller than her.

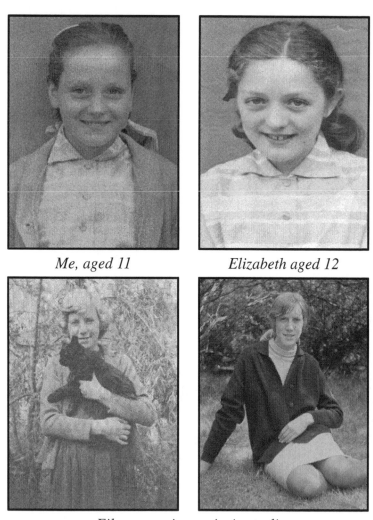

Me, aged 11   *Elizabeth aged 12*

Eileen growing up in Australia

"G'day," he said as he took her suitcase. I hoped he was not going to make comments about Aussies and corkscrew hats.

"You must be tired after your long journey," I said. "Would you like to have a coffee before we set off for home?"

"No thank you, I'm fine."

"Are you sure?" Elizabeth asked.

I couldn't quite believe that we were her big sisters. It was a new role for me. I'd always been the baby in the family.

We followed Alan to where he had parked the car.

"Would you like to sit in the front?" I asked. "You will be able to stretch your legs."

She slid into the back seat. "No, I am quite happy to sit in the back."

"Are you comfortable?" Elizabeth asked.

I pushed the front seat up. "Have you got enough room for your legs, pet?" I asked.

"Yes, thank you. I'm just fine." She was all smiles.

Alan put her large suitcase in the boot of the car and got into the drivers seat. We set off for Teesside.

I was sat in the passenger seat and could see her in the side view mirror. I tried to avoid staring at her. "How was your flight?" I asked.

She smiled. "It was good until we landed, then there were problems. The door jammed. The crew told us that they may have to bring a set of stairs to get us off the plane. There was a lot of humorous banter between the passengers waiting to get off the plane. It made me laugh. Then the luggage took some time to come through. We were waiting ages."

"Welcome to England," Alan said. "You look like your mother."

Eileen was thrilled. "Did you know her?"

"Oh yes, I knew her alright. She was a character, she liked a good time.

"Remember that time in the restaurant, Anne?"

I certainly did. I hoped he wasn't going to relate it to Eileen. Mother had come to visit us on Teesside from her home in Liverpool. She had gone out on her own. Alan and I were having a meal in a restaurant with friends when Mother came in and headed for the ladies. I could tell that she was kaylied. She could be quite aggressive when she'd had one too many. I wanted to avoid her. When I saw her I dived under the table. Alan hadn't seen her. But when he heard her shouting (luckily she hadn't seen us) he quickly followed me under the table, much to the amusement of our friends.

"I think we can tell Eileen that tale another time," I said.

"What do you think of our countryside Eileen?"

"It's lovely."

"Very similar to Australia, I should think," Alan said, "but don't the sheep outnumber people?"

"Eee, I can't stop looking at you," Elizabeth said. "You are so like our mother."

28

CHAPTER 5

Getting to know you

"Would you like a cup of tea Eileen?"

She was sitting on the settee, her long legs stretched out in front of her.

"Yes please."

"Now you don't mind cheese do you?" I asked as I made my way into the kitchen.

"That would be lovely, thank you." She was ever so nice and polite, this new sister of mine.

Elizabeth was chatting to Eileen. I took the opportunity to get Alan's attention. I needed to tell him not to say too much about Mother at this stage.

"Come on Alan, you can give me a hand." He looked at me inquisitively.

Reluctantly he got up from the sofa and followed me into the kitchen.

"Be careful what you say to her about our mam."

"Why? She's got to know the truth sometime."

"Yes, but we've got to put ourselves in her shoes. She's come all this way to meet us and she's dreamed of the day when she would meet her own mother. And that's never going to happen. Plus, she has idealistic notions about mother.

"Cut the cucumber, will you."

"Ok, I'll only say nice things about her."

"She did have her good points, you know."

29

"Such as?"

"Well, if she hadn't had me, you wouldn't have such a gorgeous wife."

"That's true."

"Ah, that's nice, pet."

"But, I'm glad that you took after your dad."

"The unknown Norwegian sailor?"

I put cheese and salad sandwiches on the coffee table. "You must be tired, Eileen?"

"I'm fine. I had a nice rest at the hotel. It refreshed me."

Alan brought in mugs of tea and coffee on a tray. "Right then, who wants tea and who wants coffee?" I hoped he wasn't expecting us to put our hands up like the kids in the classroom. He often carried on as if he was in still in school. "Lower your voice," I would remind him. "You're not in the classroom now."

Alan asked Eileen if she could see the resemblance between Elizabeth and I.

"Oh yes, definitely, especially round the eyes."

Alan agreed. "That's where I see it between the three of you."

"What colour are your eyes, Eileen?" Elizabeth asked. "Anne's eyes are bluer than mine."

I was surprised. "Are they? I never noticed."

We all looked at Eileen.

"Definitely blue," Alan said.

"Bluer than mine," I said. Elizabeth agreed.

Eileen smiled. "What colour were Mother's eyes?"

"Blue. And Grandfather had the same colour," Elizabeth said.

"Your mother used to squint when she watched the television," Alan said. "Anne does the same thing - especially when she's had one too many."

What! He's thinking that squinting at the television is a family trait passed on through the generations?

"Er, less of your cheek," I replied.

"Well it's true!" he said.

"Would anyone like another sandwich?" I asked, changing the subject.

CHAPTER 6
The first day

The alarm went off. "There's something different about today," I thought. Of course, my newly found sister was sleeping in the next room.

"Try and be quiet," I whispered to Alan as he headed for the bathroom. I sat on the side of the bed trying to take in the events of yesterday. We had talked until it was almost midnight. Alan had to get up early for work and had gone to bed about ten o'clock. Eileen and I chatted about our family and most of all about Mother, and who could blame her.

My heart was fluttering. 'Ah no, that's all I need, to have a full blown atrial fibrillation attack!' I thought. I had been diagnosed with this heart complaint about ten years earlier. Every now and then the electrical system of my heart goes awry which leads to an irregular heart rate, causing palpitations etc. I was on medication to control it. On the whole it worked, but not always, and then I would have to be hospitalized.

"I'll go downstairs and take my heart tablets," I said to Alan, although it would mean taking them one hour earlier than usual. I put on my dressing room and tiptoed past her room. I heard her moving about. She was already awake. Luckily, the palpitations eased but I decided to take my tablets anyway. Alan was going to the gym, so he collected his gear and gave me a peck on the cheek.

"Good luck. Enjoy your day with your sister," he said as he went out the front door.

I heard the bedroom door open. Eileen came down the stairs. I was in the kitchen putting the kettle on. "Hi," she said.

"Did you sleep well?" I asked.

"Yes, very well thank you. I felt so contented. When I woke up I was lying in bed thinking, I am in a house that belongs to my 'real' sister. I would never have thought it possible."

I put a bowl of porridge in the microwave. She had told me that she liked to have fruit for breakfast. I took blackberries, blueberries, strawberries and raspberries out the fridge. "Help yourself," I said as I handed her a cereal bowl. She put a mixture of fruit into it and followed me into the sitting room.

We sat at the dining table, me with my porridge coated with honey to satisfy my sweet tooth.

"You like to eat healthy," I said. "What foods do you like?"

"Salads. I could have them every day."

Now that was something we did not have in common as salads leave me cold. But we both agreed that we have a sweet tooth and chocolate was top of our list.

It was amazing how at ease we were with each other. It really was as if we had known each other all our lives.

Breakfast over, we cleared the table and took the dishes into the kitchen. She offered to help me wash up.

"No, I'm going to put this lot in the dishwasher," I said.

In the sitting room we made ourselves comfy. She sat on the three-seater settee, while I sat on the armchair. Now was the time to talk, and invariably the conversation turned to our mother.

"I wished we had found you sooner," I said. "We have been looking for you for thirty four years. We just kept hitting a brick wall. Raphy showed Elizabeth those two letters that he'd got from the registrar at Stobhill Hospital. He received them in 1951 but he kept it a secret. It was only when Elizabeth had visited him to tell him Mother had died that he'd showed her the letters. That was in 1976. Elizabeth asked him why he hadn't replied to the letters. He said that he didn't want to get involved. The story of his life, I think. He never bothered to come and see Elizabeth and I in Nazareth House. His excuse was that the nuns kept pestering him for money and he felt embarrassed when he couldn't give them anything. Still, he knew I wasn't his. Mother told him. She was brazen about it. But he can't have wanted to split the family because he was prepared to keep me and even gave me my name.

"The letter from the registrar didn't tell us if you were a boy or a girl. When we did find out that you were a girl we were over the moon. Then we saw on your birth certificate that you had been adopted. We couldn't get any more information about you. We were told that siblings had no rights. It was up to you to find us and then only if you wished. All we could do was leave our contact details with various adoption agencies and hope that one day you would contact them. But as the years went by we realised that was never going to happen. We had searched for you in the UK. I just had an inkling that you might not be in this country. But where do we look? That website was to be our last effort to find you and thanks to the person who set it up, you are here with us."

Eileen smiled.

"I should send him an email and thank him," she said.

"When I saw my name on that website I could not believe it. I must have read it a dozen times. I tried to contact the email address but I needed to go through the owner of the site. Unfortunately, I couldn't contact him. He was on holiday. I was getting desperate. I was thinking of getting a private investigator to find out who Elizabeth Traynor was. Fortunately this guy called Paul emailed me Marie's email address and here I am."

"Mother must have wanted you to trace her one day. That is why she gave you both her maiden name and her married name.

"We might have thought better of Mother if we had known that she was pregnant with you. We just thought that she had left because she didn't want to be tied down with us. It makes sense why she walked out. Whether she intended to come back for us we will never know. Maybe she thought that we were better off in Nazareth House, especially when she came to see us.

"Raphy didn't keep us for long either. Ten days later he put Elizabeth and I in Nazareth House."

"And we had a brother, Denis?" she asked.

"Yes."

I had emailed her a photograph of Denis. It was taken when he was in the Royal Air Force. He has one knee on the ground and a broad smile on his face. There are two friends standing either side of him.

Dennis (centre) in the RAF.

"Elizabeth and I think that he suffered the most with the breakup of the family. He was 13 years of age at the time. He came with us when we were dropped off at Nazareth House, but then left with Raphy. Imagine what it would have felt like leaving his sisters in that place."

Eileen sighed. "It must have been awful for him."

"Elizabeth and I had just got in contact with him and were getting to know him when he was murdered. It was such a shock and he was only thirty nine."

"Poor Denny," Eileen said.

I had told Eileen about the circumstances of his death before she came over from Australia so that she would be prepared for when we spoke about it. Then hopefully it would not come as too much of a shock, although there was no easy way to soften the blow.

"You have traced the family tree?"

"Yes, it took me ages. It wasn't cheap either sending for all those certificates. It was difficult as I had to start from scratch. All I knew was that Mother was born in Glasgow and that her mother had died in 1943 before Elizabeth and I were born. Grandfather George lived in Hawick, that's where he was born and brought up, but it seems that he had come to Glasgow as an adult and had settled down there. The first thing I did was to send for our mother's birth certificate and through that I found Grandmother's maiden name. She was called Mary Hair. Grandmother's parents were called Janet and John. They lived in an area of Glasgow called Kinning

Park and were married in the Kinning Park Parish Church. I sent for their marriage and death certificates and I found that we have heart disease in the family. I often wondered if this is why I got atrial fibrillation at such a young age. It started to really affect me when I hit my early fifties and that is when I needed treatment for it.

"The cardiologist asked me if there was any heart disease in the family. That was before I knew about our family history. I had to tell him that I hadn't a clue. I think that was one of the reasons I decided to do the research to find out just what medical conditions we may have inherited.

"Elizabeth and I thought you also should know about our medical background. It was another good reason to find you."

Eileen agreed. "I remember going to the doctors when I was a teenager. He asked my mother about my medical history. She had to tell the doctor that she didn't know. That was an awkward moment."

"Ah well, at least we know now. Elizabeth and I have decided to let you have a few days rest to recuperate from your long journey before we travel up to Scotland."

"Ooh that would be lovely. I am looking forward to getting my adoption papers and seeing the place where I was born."

"I hope we get to see the roads where our relations lived."

"That would be wonderful."

"Elizabeth and I have arranged it all. We are your big sisters, pet, we have to look after you."

She smiled, crossed her legs and smoothed her skirt down just like Mother would have done.

CHAPTER 7

DNA

A few weeks beforehand, I had arranged for Eileen and I to have a DNA test. Although Elizabeth and I had no doubt that Eileen was our mother's daughter, I wanted the test done to find out if we could be full sisters. I did not know who my father was and there was a slight chance that we may have had the same father, albeit a small one. Elizabeth and I'd had a DNA test done previously and it had proved that we shared the same mother but not the father. We knew that Elizabeth was Raphy's daughter as she looks like him. This DNA test would reassure Eileen and prove that we were related.

It was an important day for us as it would prove beyond doubt that we were siblings. It would also give Eileen evidence she did indeed belong to our family. I remember that it was a grey rainy day but I was happy and optimistic as having seen her I didn't doubt that she was our sister. And she looked so like our Mother. We got the bus to Stockton-on-Tees and then took a taxi to the clinic.

On arrival we were greeted warmly by a lady and taken into a room. I had spoken to this lady over the phone and had told her why we wanted the test done. She was fascinated when I told her that we had found out about Eileen only after our mother had died. She said that it was a lot easier if a parent could be tested along with any children, but this was not possible as both our mother and father were deceased. It was such a simple procedure. She simply used cotton wool to swab the inside of our cheeks. Each sample was then put into its own container and sent off to the laboratory. We were informed that it might take up to three weeks for the results to come back but she hoped that Eileen would receive them before she returned to Australia. Afterwards we went out with a friend and had a celebratory lunch in a café in Norton.

CHAPTER 8
Train Journey

A week after Eileen's arrival, we headed for the railway station at Thornaby to catch the early morning train to Edinburgh. When the train arrived Eileen struggled to get her large case in the small space between the seats. Elizabeth's case was almost as large as Eileen's but hers had no wheels attached so she had to carry it along the narrow aisles. "We're only going for five days Elizabeth," I said. We all laughed.

I was travelling light and I carried my small case down the aisle.

"Bet the trains in Australia are roomier than these, Eileen?"

"They are."

"Is that because they have to transport all those sheep?" She laughed.

I managed to get two seats - one for me another for my case. Elizabeth and Eileen had to leave their cases in the passageway.

The three of us sat down and breathed a sigh of relief.

The train started up, slowly at first then gathered momentum. I looked around the carriage. There were only a few passengers on the train but at each stop along the way we picked up more whom I assumed were on their way to work. All three of us were in separate seats, near enough to see

42

each other, but if we wanted to talk we had to lean over and shout.

On the seat opposite was a young woman. She was wearing a smart suit, her fair hair tied up. I could only see the side of her face as she was texting on her mobile phone.

The seat in front of her was occupied by a middle aged man. He was balancing a laptop precariously on his knee, holding on with one hand as he typed on the keyboard. In the double seats in front of me sat an elderly woman. She was chatting incessantly to the middle aged woman sitting by her side. The other woman didn't speak, just nodded her head like a Churchill dog in a car window.

The ticket collector came round. "Tickets please," he said. There was a mass fumble in pockets and handbags. I handed him the three tickets and he took them, clipping a piece of each ticket.

"Change at Darlington," he barked as he handed them back to me. We stopped at Northallerton Station where a man in overalls got on and plonked his haversack on an empty seat before sitting down. The train set off. I sat there for a while looking out of the window, wondering what we would find out about Eileen's adoption.

Suddenly the train came to a halt. I looked out of the window but all I could see were green fields. The train had come to a standstill in the middle of the countryside.

"Why have we stopped here?" the elderly woman asked.

There were murmurings among other passengers.

I leaned over the side of the seat. "I don't know why we've stopped," I said to Elizabeth and Eileen.

The ticket collector came back into the compartment.

"Sorry to have to inform you but we've had to stop the train. There has been an incident just outside Darlington."

"How long are we expected to remain here?" the man with the laptop asked.

"Couldn't tell you, mate. I've just been given this message."

The middle aged woman was anxious. "We've got to get to the airport," she said. "We've a plane to catch, we're going to a wedding."

"I've got a meeting to go to," the young lady said.

We were not far from Darlington, so the man with the laptop asked, "Can you let me off? I'll walk to the station."

"Can't do that, mate. Health and safety, and its more than me job's worth."

"How long will we have to wait?" he replied.

"Dunno mate." The ticket collector tapped in a number on his mobile.

He made his way along the narrow aisle to the other compartment, where you could hear him repeating himself. "Dunno mate, waiting for confirmation."

"I wonder what's happened?" the young girl asked.

"Maybe it's been a suicide, that's why they call them incidents," the man in overalls suggested.

"Ooh how awful," the elderly woman piped up. "Bet it's a young man, the poor soul. What a tragedy for his family."

"It might not be a young man," the man in overalls responded. "I heard a young woman jumped in front of a train after she'd given birth. She had that depression that you get after giving birth."

"Not everyone gets depressed after giving birth. I didn't," the elderly woman said. "Didn't have time, just had to get on with it. And you were such a cry baby," she said to the middle aged woman sitting at her side.

"Ah thanks, tell the world will you."

The man in overalls laughed. "I got depressed 'cos I couldn't have me nights out with the lads."

The old woman tutted. "That's all you men think about."

"Shush, be quiet Mother," her daughter said.

The ticket collector arrived back into our compartment.

"Right then, where is everyone going to? We may have to put on a mini bus."

"We have to change trains at Darlington," I said. "We're going to Edinburgh."

"I have to change at Darlington as well," the young lass said. "I have to catch a train to London."

"My, you have a long journey ahead," I said.

"I'll be making a return journey tonight," she replied.

"You'll be shattered."

"I enjoy travelling," she said. "It's part of my job."

The middle aged woman was reading an article about Bob Geldof.

"I've heard that he's dead rude," she said. "My friend's daughter asked him for his autograph and he ignored her, totally blanked her, he did. He swears a lot an' all. He swore when he was on Live Aid."

The young woman defended him. I wondered if she knew him?

"He's lovely, really. He probably didn't mean to ignore her but when he's in a hurry to get anywhere and he gets stopped he can get narked, but wouldn't anyone?"

"Not if I had his money, I wouldn't," the middle aged woman said. "I'd be grateful for my fans. And with all that money he's got, you'd think he could afford to get his hair cut."

"He's done a lot for Live Aid," the man in overalls said. "Saved all those bairns lives, he did. He's a saint."

"Saint Bob?" I asked.

Laptop man was wondering whether he should take his chance and get off the train. But just then the ticket collector came back and informed us that the incident was in the process of being cleared.

"It's just a lorry, it got stuck under a bridge."

Was that all?

CHAPTER 9
Edinburgh

We changed trains at Darlington and had a sandwich and a coffee at the station cafeteria before catching the Edinburgh bound service.

On board we had plenty of room to stretch our legs and we chatted as the train passed through some fantastic scenery. The air seemed to get fresher the further north we went. Eventually, the train pulled into Edinburgh Waverley Station.

"I can't believe I am actually in Scotland," Eileen said.

We got off the train. I looked around. Mother must have been here many times. We had to take the lift and with our luggage squeezed in beside us we made our way to the upper floor. We got out of the lift, but there were more stairs to climb.

"You have to be fit to live here. Everything is uphill," Elizabeth said.

Elizabeth and Eileen dragged their
cases up the stairs. A young man stopped to help.

We reached the main road. I put my arm out to stop a taxi but they whizzed past us.

"Don't think they are going to stop," I said. "We may have to book one."

"Eileen, show a leg, pet. You have such nice long ones."

We managed to stop a black taxi cab and with our cases on board we headed for The Belford Guest House at Newington.

13 Blacket Avenue, Edinburgh.

Eileen had told me that this was the house where she had lived with her adopted parents before they had immigrated to Australia when she was four years old. I found out via the internet that it was now a guest house.

I'd booked us in for three days. She was thrilled when I told her.

The taxi took us down a leafy lane and stopped at 13 Blacket Avenue.

The driver dropped our cases at the door. We gave him a tip.

Eileen was all smiles. She stood at the gate looking up at the windows. "It's just as I remember it," she said.

The door opened and an elderly man appeared. He said that the owner Tom was out at the moment. He was Tom's father in law.

I told him that we three sisters had a booking.

We were given a key to the front door plus two keys to get into our rooms.

"Your rooms are on the top floor," he said. "I'm sorry that I can't help you carry the cases but I have a bad back." Oh no, more stairs and there was no lift. We hauled our cases up three flights of stairs giggling like school girls.

"It's like climbing Ben Nevis," I said. We had to keep stopping for a rest. I was knackered and we had two more flights of stairs to go but after much huffing and puffing we got there.

I had booked a family room with en-suite for Eileen. Elizabeth and I would be sharing a double room with a separate bathroom. It had twin beds a double wardrobe and a small washbasin. It was clean and comfy.

Eileen's room overlooked the back garden.

"What do you think then, Eileen, of your old home?"

"I don't think I came up to this part of the house, but the back garden looks familiar."

I looked out of the window. "It's so high up it's giving me vertigo."

We helped ourselves to tea and coffee and the chocolate biscuits that Tom had laid out for us.

Elizabeth said she hadn't enough coat hangers and was going to go downstairs and ask for a few more.

"What, you're going to make that trek back up here just for a few coat hangers?" I said. I had to admire her.

I joked that Elizabeth seemed to have brought the whole contents of her wardrobe from home.

It was now after midday and we were feeling hungry. We decided to venture out and find some place to eat. We made our way down the stairs. It was much easier than going up them but I was tempted to slide down the nice polished banister.

Elizabeth and I have dodgy right arthritic knees. I wonder if it runs in the family. Eileen didn't have the same problem, though.

"You're younger than us, pet," I told her. "You can take your pick between having an irregular heart rate, which I seem to have inherited from our Scots granny or an underactive thyroid like Elizabeth."

"I've had my gall bladder removed," she said.

"Oh, so did Mother. You've not escaped the family ailments then."

Tom only did breakfasts so there was no chance of being fed. He suggested various places. "Just follow the road downhill," he advised. Downhill? That sounded good. We thanked him and off we went.

We set off down a quiet, leafy walkway. We turned the corner and further down the road we came to the Lord Salisbury. It looked rather grand. Inside there were wide comfy chairs to lounge in and most importantly there were no stairs.

"We'll come in here," I said. The waitress led us to a table set for three. They must have been expecting us, I thought. I looked at the menu. It was not cheap but who cared. It's not every day that you have a meal with a long lost sister. I chose the specialty meal of the day - after all it was a special occasion.

We enjoyed a long leisurely lunch and talked about the plans we had for the following day.

"It's D-day tomorrow, Eileen," I said. "You'll find out who your father is. How do you feel about that?"

"I'm both excited and nervous," she said.

After paying the bill we strolled back to the Belford, the three of us thinking about what tomorrow would bring. I just hoped that it would give Eileen the answers that she was seeking.

CHAPTER 10
The Belford

That night I lay in a warm, cosy bed while the wind howled and rattled the windows. I thought of our mother.

What would she have said if she had known that Elizabeth and I would find the baby girl that she gave up for adoption sixty years ago? How would she have reacted? Raphy had carried those two letters in his wallet for all those years. If he hadn't shown them to Elizabeth we would never have known about Eileen. I was eternally grateful to him for that.

In the morning we came down for breakfast. Tom was in the kitchen cooking breakfast for the couple sat at a table in the dining room. We wished them good morning. They were American and from New Hampshire.

Tom came in with their breakfasts. He was looking hot and bothered.

"Phew, it's hot in there," he said. "What do you want for breakfast?"

I asked for porridge, but Tom looked aghast when I told him I liked to sweeten it with honey.

"The Scots put salt on theirs," he explained. I decided to do the same. When in Rome etc. I tasted it. No, I much preferred it with honey. But the porridge itself was delicious.

Elizabeth opted for a traditional full Scottish breakfast. It was a good fry up which looked much the same as we have in England. Tom claimed that it wasn't the same, though, as the Scottish version was much better. I agreed. "Of course it is Tom."

Tom took his time, overwhelmed by all the cooking. He came into the dining room carrying the breakfasts. The large beef tomatoes had burnt, fluted edges. We pretended not to notice.

It was nice to have a man cooking breakfast for us. I really should give Alan cookery lessons.

We asked Tom for the number of a taxi to take us to the centre.

"It's only down the road," he said. "You can walk it in ten minutes."

Not with our dodgy knees. Elizabeth telephoned for a taxi. It arrived complete with a handsome friendly driver. He politely opened the doors for each of us.

Eileen sat in the front while I sat behind the driver. We told him that we were heading for the Edinburgh Registry Office. He said he would drop us off just across the road as it was the nearest he could go.

"Are you on holiday?" he asked.

We told him that we were researching our family history and that we would be going to Glasgow in a couple of days. There was a friendly rivalry between the Edinburghs and the Glaswegians, he admitted.

"I'd like my children to know more about their Scottish roots," I said. I told him that my sons could be eligible to play for Scotland as they had a Scottish granny but said there were quite a few in England though who didn't think that

Scotland had a football team. Oops! I assured him I was only kidding.

CHAPTER 11

General Register for Scotland

The taxi dropped us off near the Balmoral Hotel. We gave the driver a tip. It was very windy and a light rain was falling as we made our way along Princes Street. It was bustling with people of all nationalities.

We linked arms as we crossed the busy road. We were heading for the large grey building where Eileen's adoption papers were situated.

There was a statue of a man on a horse. It was the Duke of Wellington. I wondered why there was a monument to him. Wasn't he an Englishman? Nearby, a lone piper was playing the bagpipes. People were dropping money into a box at his feet.

I love the sound of bagpipes. I was tempted to stop and listen for a while but it was very windy and besides we had more important things to do.

We arrived at the building and looked for the adoptions department.

We entered a large wooden door and approached the man sitting at the reception desk.

"Can I help you?" he asked. I took a deep breath. At last we were going to find out the truth of her adoption. I explained that Eileen had come to see her adoption papers.

Eileen gave her pre-adoption name, date of birth and the year she was born. We were told to sit in the waiting room.

Eileen was pleased that we were there with her. "I would not have liked to have done this on my own," she admitted.

"We could be ages, they have to search back to 1951," I said. I hoped that they hadn't lost the vital papers.

Elizabeth admitted to feeling a bit nervous. I was excited, looking forward to finding out things. Eileen said she felt okay.

Eventually a woman arrived suggesting we go somewhere more private. We followed her down a long corridor and through some double doors. She unlocked a door and we entered a large room. It must have been used for meetings as there was a long table with chairs around it. She sat down and we sat facing her. She looked from one to another. "My name is Fiona. How can I help you?"

Where to start? We told her about Eileen's adoption, about her emigration to Australia and how we found out about her after our mother had died. We explained that the three of us have all got different fathers and that Elizabeth and I were brought up in an orphanage run by nuns.

Fiona got quite emotional as we related our story. "I'm so pleased you found each other," she said as she wiped a tear from her eye.

"You do look alike," she said. "I can see the resemblance around the eyes." We agreed.

"I feel that I had a happy upbringing compared to my sisters," Eileen said.

Fiona took us to the adoptions department. It was in another part of the building.

"It may take some time to find the documents," she warned. "I suggest you have some lunch and come back this afternoon. There is a cafeteria within the building."

We went through more double doors and found a self service café. We helped ourselves to sandwiches. Elizabeth and Eileen had a coffee. I plumped for a hot chocolate - I needed my sugar fix.

"Hope we didn't upset Fiona too much," Eileen said. "She was quite amazed when we told her our story."

I agreed. "She must get to hear some harrowing tales and probably on a daily basis but I think that she was taken aback by ours."

We went back to the adoptions area and waited in the reception. Fiona came to tell us that she hadn't located the documents yet but would keep searching.

"She'll probably have to look in the archives," Eileen joked.

I was starting to get restless. There was a tourist stand nearby and I picked out a few leaflets. They were all about the attractions on offer in Edinburgh. There was the Castle, Holyrood Palace and Greyfriars Bobby.

I showed them to Eileen. "Ah, I must see the statue of Greyfriars wee dog," she said. "I'd love a photograph to take back to Australia."

We agreed that we must do a bus tour of Edinburgh before we left.

There was a seat near the reception area which I plonked myself down on. "How long have you worked here then?" I asked the male receptionist.

"Long enough," he replied. His name was Neil and he seemed a friendly chap. We soon got chatting away and we told him the reason we were there. He told us about a letter that was addressed to a Mr. John Waldie. It was found behind a fireplace in a house in Edinburgh. We wondered if there might be any connection to us.

The hours passed. I hoped that Fiona would find the adoption papers today. I didn't fancy coming back again the next day. Elizabeth worried that we may have to. Neil asked us where we came from. "Middlesbrough, it's in the North East," I told him.

"Middlesbrough?"

"Don't mention the football team," I joked. "I think they're hovering around the bottom of the league, that seems to be their favourite spot."

"We call it the 'Boro' for short," Elizabeth said.

Neil had heard of it but didn't think he had been there. "You would know if you had," I said.

"Edinburgh has all these fabulous monuments but I think that the Boro can compete. We have something called the Bottle of Notes. It's a work of art that's situated in the Centre Square near the Town Hall and it's over thirty feet high." Neil looked puzzled.

"Google it and you'll see what I'm talking about."

It came up on the screen. "What's the significance of it?" he asked.

"It's something to do with our industrial heritage," I told him proudly, "and there's an extract from Captain James Cook's log book engraved on it. And Redcar is only down the road from us. They filmed Atonement there. It starred Kiera Knightly and Scottish actor James McAvoy. Those war scenes were done on Redcar Beach. And we also have a new vertical pier. Everyone calls it the Helter Skelter."

"Why?"

"It resembles one."

He googled 'Vertical Pier,' and it popped up instantly. Guess it must be the only vertical pier in the world.

"And in Stockton-on-Tees we have the widest high street in the country. It takes ages to get from one side to the other." Alright, "I was exaggerating," I admitted.

"See? We're quite famous," I told him. I was doing my bit to promote our area.

Fiona came to the reception area. She hadn't found the documents yet but she remained confident. We decided to go for some fresh air and browse the shops.

It was blowing a gale along Princes Street. We scarpered into a tourist shop selling lots of tartan souvenirs. Eileen said she loved black faced sheep as they don't have many in Australia. We looked to see if there was any in the shop (not the real ones). There was a poster showing all the different clans and the various tartans belonging to them. I searched for our family name, Waldie, but it wasn't there.

"You will probably come under the auspices of one of the bigger clans," the shop assistant said. I was deflated that our clan was quite insignificant. "We were probably immigrants," I said to Eileen.

Eileen found a black faced sheep. She was delighted and added it to her growing collection of souvenirs.

There was a cafeteria in the shop but it was upstairs. We climbed the stairs - there were a lot of them but the aroma of hot dinners kept us going. The place was almost full to capacity but the waitress managed to find us a table. There were spectacular views of the castle and surrounding area. It was well worth the climb.

We chose cheese and ham sandwiches and scones with jam and cream. All this climbing had given us an appetite.

"Sorry you have to wait so long to get your documents," I said to Eileen.

"I've waited years," she said. "If I have to wait a few hours more I don't mind."

We sauntered back to the registry. There was a lone piper standing by the statue of Wellington. We dropped some money in the box. Eileen asked if she could take his photograph. "Happy to oblige," he said. It was very windy, and I got to thinking that if we stood here for much longer we would soon discover what a Scotsman wears under his kilt.

CHAPTER 12
Unlocking the past

"I've found the documents," a smiling Fiona said.

"Follow me," she ordered as she led us down a corridor. We were taken into a small side room and we sat at a table in the corner of the room. We were like children, excitedly waiting to receive a birthday present. How many adoptees had sat here in anticipation, waiting to hear the details of their adoption?

Fiona left the room, and when she returned she was wearing gloves and holding a cardboard box.

She opened it and took out a large brown package. It was sealed and had a red stamp on the back. She handed it to Eileen. It smelled foisty as it hadn't been opened since 1952. There were quite a few papers inside.

Eileen picked up the first paper, read it then passed it to me and Elizabeth. There were documents of the court proceedings regarding the adoption, details about the prospective adopted parents and a copy of Eileen's birth certificate.

We passed the papers between us as we read each one in turn. There was quiet in the room as we took in what was on the pages. We found out where Mother had been living at the time. Elizabeth and I laughed when it said that she was working as a shoe sales lady.

There was a copy of a letter that Mother had written. Elizabeth and I recognized her hand writing.

64 Polworth St
Hynland
Glasgow
8/1/52

Dear Sir,

With reference to your letter regarding my child Eileen Mary.

I have never taken any legal proceedings against the father although parentage was admitted as he filled the form for adoption. Only reason for not taking any proceedings against him as he is a well known professional business man and myself being in a good position. I therefore wanted no scandal what-so-ever.

Yours faithfully

Mary Traynor.

There was no mention of Eileen's father. We were disappointed for Eileen.

The paper stated that Eileen had been born at 133 Balornock Road, Glasgow.

But we'd always though Eileen had been born in Stobhill Hospital. It was rather odd.

Fiona said that she would photocopy all the papers that were enclosed in the package. This would mean that the three of us would have all the details of Eileen's adoption, which was very thoughtful of her.

Meanwhile we three discussed the documents of the package.

Was Eileen's father really some anonymous businessman? The papers stated that the address Mother had given was the same one where a certain Hugh Clark had also been living. Mother often spoke about this guy, but Elizabeth and I had never met him.

We learned that Eileen's adopted parents were desperate to have her. They had written a letter to the court. They had to have their home inspected and approved. It was the very same house that we were staying in at the moment. It received a favourable report (although I would have recommended installing a stair lift). It seemed that Mother knew exactly who was to adopt Eileen and where she would be living. Eileen was pleased about that.

Fiona said that we could come back the next day and use the family research facilities if we wished.

Back at the Belford we went through the papers again.

"Mother said that she was a shoe sales assistant," Elizabeth said. "I can't believe that."

I wondered if Hugh Clark was Eileen's father.

Elizabeth disagreed. "I don't think so. Why would he agree to the adoption? Surely he would want to keep his own child."

"Yes, that's a thought, and then what about you and me, Elizabeth? Do you think Mother would have taken us out of Nazareth House and brought us to Scotland to live with her?"

"I very much doubt it."

"Mother said he was a businessman and she did tell us that Hugh Clark was a journalist. I wonder when she met him?"

I was surprised to learn that she was living in Glasgow with him when the adoption took place.

Mother was pregnant when she left Middlesbrough so that ruled out Hugh Clark as the father.

We couldn't ask him either because he was dead. Mother told me she'd seen his obituary in the newspaper.

Well, who was her father?

CHAPTER 13
Tour of Edinburgh

We came down for breakfast the next morning. There were two women sat at a table in the dining room. We politely wished them good morning. They were American, a mother and daughter from Texas. It seemed Tom was popular with the Yanks. It must be the porridge.

We informed Tom that we had decided to go on a tour bus and see the sights of Edinburgh.

He served us a delicious full Scottish breakfast. "This will set you up for the day," he said.

The American ladies wanted to go to Princes Street. They wondered if they should get a taxi. "It's not far to walk," Tom said.

The younger woman tapped in the directions on her mobile.

"It's miles away," she disagreed. We gave her the taxi number.

Elizabeth ordered a taxi and soon another handsome, friendly driver arrived to take us to Princes Street.

On Waverley Bridge we boarded the Hop-on Hop-off tour bus. It was windy but the sun was threatening to break through. We went inside to get out of the wind. The bus soon filled with excited tourists with cameras at the ready.

Greyfriars Bobby, Edinburgh

The bus set off. The first stop was the Scott's Monument. This large Gothic construction was dedicated to Walter Scott, Scotland's famous writer.

Eileen had read his novel Ivanhoe.

In Nazareth House we would look forward to watching Ivanhoe on the television. A young Roger Moore was the knight in shining armour. He rode a white horse and his helmet had an enormous plume of white feathers. It was probably over the top but it looked rather grand on the old black and white television.

Eileen took plenty of photographs as the bus slowly made its way round the city.

"I can look at them when I'm back in Australia," she said. "It will remind me of the wonderful time I've had with my sisters."

We got off the bus on the Royal Mile. There was a good atmosphere and the sun had broken through. Tourists with their cameras were snapping everything in sight and in the distance we heard the sound of bagpipes. We sauntered along looking in the many shops while taking in the sights and sounds. We came to the castle esplanade that was in front of the gateway to the castle. This is where the annual Military Edinburgh Tattoo is held. There was seating on either side. I'd watched it so many times on the television. The space was smaller than I'd imagined. Eileen said she'd also seen it on television in Australia. "How do they get all those marching bands in such a small area?" I wondered.

There was a placard which commemorates the large number of women burned as witches on this spot.

They didn't stand a chance dunked in the river and if they drowned they were innocent. If they didn't drown they were guilty and burnt at the stake.

That law was definitely man-made.

We decided not to walk around the castle but there was a fantastic view overlooking Edinburgh. In the distance we saw people walking up and down Princes Street.

In the castle gift shop I purchased a Scottish piper teddy bear for my granddaughter in New Zealand.

We ambled back down the Royal Mile until we came to an arched alleyway leading to James Court. There was a placard with an arrow pointing the way to the Jolly Judge.

Curious, I suggested we take a look. We went down the stone steps.

We were not disappointed. The pub turned out to be a cosy little hideaway. It had a low beamed ceiling and pastoral pictures on the walls. It was busy but we had no problem finding a seat. The landlord informed us that the pub was named after a famous judge of bygone days.

On the wall was a picture of the judge with a red nose and cheeks. That's why he looked so jolly, he'd had a skinful.

We pitied the poor prisoner who had come before this judge. Especially if he had a hangover.

We ate our meal and talked about the events of yesterday.

I wondered if Mother had married this Hugh Clark. She talked about him often enough.

"Denis told me that she got a regular allowance from him," Elizabeth said.

It got me thinking. Had she married him while she was still married to Raphy? I was determined to find out.

In the meantime we decided to enjoy ourselves.

The statue of Greyfriars Bobby was located close to the George IV Bridge. The tourists were crowding round the statue, taking photographs and rubbing the nose of the dog. I wondered if it was a ritual.

68

"Why do they do that?" I asked.

"It's for luck," a woman replied in a broad American accent.

"Ees very good," a Chinese girl said as she posed for the camera. Seems they were all interested in the story of the wee terrier that had remained by its master's grave for fourteen years.

I took a few photos of Eileen posing with the statue before going to the Greyfriars Kirkyard.

We entered the Kirkyard cemetery where many famous Scots are buried but none more renowned than Bobby.

Mother was buried in Liverpool. I told Eileen she had lived there for over twenty years. I felt quite sad that she was buried many miles away from the place of her birth.

We boarded the red tour bus and arrived back on Waverley Bridge. It was time for some retail therapy and we crossed over to the shopping centre. We sauntered around the shops but I suppose all town centres are similar. There were the usual Marks and Spencer and New Look etc. We didn't want to be burdened down with more stuff as we could purchase the items nearer to home. But we bought souvenirs and Eileen got some postcards to send to Australia.

Back at the Belford we trekked up the stairs with our mementos. We must have been getting fitter as I only stopped the once for a rest. I lay on the bed. It had been a good but tiring day.

We were moving on to Glasgow the next day. To celebrate our stay in Edinburgh we had fish and chips at our favourite venue, the Lord Shaftesbury. We talked about wee Bobby. "I have a photo of Mother with a black Labrador," Elizabeth said, "but she herself preferred cats and had one called Tabitha who had lived to a ripe old age." Eileen said that she had taken in many stray cats. I arrived at the conclusion that we were a family of animal lovers.

Back at the Belford we reminded Tom's father in law that we were leaving in the morning. We told him that Eileen used to live here. He gave us a tour of the house and the garden, which brought back a lot of memories for her. Eileen was thrilled to find that most of the original features still remained. She was amused to see the sculptured faces below the ceiling. They would have been around when she was living there. Somebody had painted them with rouge cheeks, blue eye shadow and ruby red lips. She laughed. "They've had a makeover," she said.

CHAPTER 14
Glasgow

The next morning the taxi arrived to take us to Glasgow. We would be staying at the Sandyford Hotel. I'd booked accommodation there because it was on Sauchiehall Street.

Mother had often mentioned Sauchiehall Street when reminiscing about her childhood. The name itself had me enthralled. "Sauchiehall? What an unusual name," I'd said. Mother knew this area very well. She was born in Glasgow and had lived in the city until her father George took up a position as an engineer in India and had moved his family there. She had come back to the city to have Eileen, then lived here for a few years.

It was a lovely sunny day when we arrived at the Sandyford. I had booked us in for two days. Elizabeth and I would be sharing a room and there was a single room for Eileen.

"Your rooms are on the first floor," the receptionist said as she handed over the keys.

"Where's the lift?" I enquired.

There wasn't one.

Ooh no, more stairs. We dragged our cases up them.

Our room was tidy with crisp white sheets on the beds. I unpacked quickly. I didn't want to waste any time. We were on a mission to explore the city and walk in Mother's footsteps.

I knocked on Eileen's door. She was pleased with her room also and it overlooked Sauchiehall Street.

I wanted to find Saint Philomena's Church so I needed the phone number. The receptionist was very helpful and found it for me. She allowed me to use the phone at reception rather than the public phone.

I rang the presbytery and a priest answered. I explained that I wanted a copy of Eileen's baptismal certificate. He was retired and was not the parish priest but said that he would look for it and get back to me. I gave him the phone number of the Sandyford.

All this travelling had given us an appetite. The receptionist suggested we try Starvin Marvins. "It's just across the road," she said. "You'll get good food there at a reasonable price."

Starving Marvin? Who the heck is he?

I looked up and down Sauchiehall Street and there were old red sandstone tenements on either side. What stories they could tell? I felt a sense of belonging, although I had never set foot in the city before.

I was quite envious of Eileen.

"Wish I'd been born in Glasgow," I told her.

We went across to Starvin Marvins.

There was a man serving behind the counter.

"Are you Marvin?" I asked.

He gave me a blank look.

"Well I thought Marvin would be named after the owner."

I was told that there was a chain of shops called Starvin Marvins. I was left feeling quite sheepish. "Well, they're not on Teesside," I said.

We came out carrying homemade soup, sandwiches and ham rolls. We intended to take them to our rooms in the Sandyford but that meant climbing those stairs. We decided to eat our lunch in the lobby instead.

It was a hot day and the windows were open so there was a wasp buzzing around us. Unfortunately, just when Elizabeth opened her sandwich the wasp landed on her hair. She has very long, thick wavy hair and the wasp got lost in it. She panicked and the sandwich and soup went up in the air much to the amusement of the hotel staff. Maybe they were not so amused when they had to clean it all up.

After lunch we decided to visit the place where Eileen was born.

"Stobhill Hospital's in Springburn," the receptionist said.

"Stob -Hill? Now, it's not on a hill?" I was thinking of my knees.

"I will order you a taxi if you like?"

When the taxi came the driver politely wished us good afternoon as he opened the doors.

Eileen commented, "How courteous the taxi drivers are."

It was very warm in the taxi and the windows were open.

Old Stobhill Hospital, Glasgow

Me and Michael at Old Stobhill Hospital, Glasgow

Ooh no, that blinkin' wasp had followed us. It was buzzing around us.

Elizabeth sat on one side of the car holding on to her hair. Eileen was sitting in the middle wafting her hand. The wasp made a beeline for the window but it nearly knocked itself out and landed on my shoulder. I was trying to keep calm as the car sped up the motorway. It started climbing up the window, buzzing frantically. It was on death row as far as I was concerned but our gentle Eileen carefully lifted her handbag up to enable it to fly out of the window. Phew!

We arrived at Stobhill Hospital but it looked nothing like the hospital I had seen on the internet. It was very modern.

"This is not Stobhill Hospital."

The taxi driver looked puzzled until we informed him we were looking for the hospital where Eileen was born.

"Most of the old one has been demolished," he explained, "but the Clock Tower is still standing. Hop in and I will take you there."

We didn't have to go far before we saw what was left of the old building. The Clock Tower stood tall and proud, but most of the hospital had been demolished. There were only a few of the old outside buildings still standing.

Eileen wondered where the actual maternity ward was?

We took photographs of Eileen outside the old entrance with the Clock Tower in the background. There were workmen at the back of the building.

I hoped they were not thinking of demolishing that wonderful old Clock Tower.

"We'll have to buy it and ship it to Australia, then you'll have a permanent reminder of where you were born."

"That would be wonderful," Eileen said.

I was thinking of Mother. What were her thoughts when she came here to have the baby? Was she thinking about Elizabeth and me? Did she know that Raphy had put us in Nazareth House?

How soon after the birth did she walk out? Was she in turmoil? So many unanswered questions.

We stood awhile looking at the remaining buildings. A man came round the corner wearing overalls. I asked him if he knew where the old maternity hospital once stood.

"I am the caretaker and have been for the last thirty years," he said. His name was Michael and there was only him and another guy to look after the place now. "What's left is going to be demolished soon," he revealed.

We told him that Eileen was born here and bombarded him with questions. He seemed enamoured by us. After all, it's not every day that you get three gorgeous women - two Sassenachs and an Aussie - hanging on to your every word.

"The maternity hospital used to be down there," he said, pointing off into the distance. It was demolished in 1992.

He invited us into what used to be the laundry but now served as his workplace. He pointed out the large pipes overhead that would have powered the various machines. "It was such a noisy place," he recalled, "you could barely see each other in the mist when all the machines were on the go." I remembered the laundry at Nazareth House so I could imagine what it would have been like.

There were sepia photographs on the wall which showed Stobhill as it was in its heyday. "In the old days we used to be self sufficient and grew our own food," he said proudly as he related the history of the hospital. There was a map showing the railway line that snaked around the outside of the hospital carrying the badly wounded soldiers from the battlefields of the First World War to the hospital.

Eileen was taking photographs both inside and outside. We took photos of Michael, to us he was a celebrity. We should have asked for his autograph. These precious mementos she would take back with her to Australia.

I asked Michael why it said 133 Balornock Road on Eileen's birth certificate, as surely it should say Stobhill Hospital? He explained that Stobhill was known as the paupers hospital, but that would stigmatise the children born here so it was decided to put the postal address down on their birth certificate.

Eileen was quite amused. "So I was born in a pauper's hospital!"

After gleaning a wealth of information from Michael we said our goodbyes to our new friend. He had been so helpful.

We took one last look at the tall red brick Clock Tower and hoped that it would not be demolished.

But we were pleased that we got to see it and the remnants of what was left of the hospital before it was too late.

CHAPTER 15
Glasgow bus tour

The next morning we came downstairs for breakfast. The dining room was in the basement. There was a variety of food to eat and we made the most of it. We were going to do the bus tour of Glasgow.

It was raining but fortunately there was a bus stop practically outside the hotel. There was a poster of Neil Oliver in the bus shelter, who had been the guide for previous bus tours. Was he going to do the live commentary? He was also the presenter of the Coast programme on television. Eileen said she had seen it in Australia.

The open topped bus arrived. It was another hop-on hop-off, only we didn't intend doing any hopping off, well not in this rain. I was looking forward to being driven around and seeing all the sights that Glasgow had to offer.

We purchased our tickets from the driver and stayed downstairs. There were not many passengers on board and no sign of Neil Oliver. The bus set off down Sauchiehall Street and we passed Buchanan Street where the lawyer who dealt with Eileen's adoption had his offices in 1952. We had seen the address on the adoption papers.

The bus took us to George Square where there were lots of statues. That's what I loved about this city, it celebrated its history, its entrepreneurs, architects, writers and royalty. I would have loved Grandfather to have accompanied us. Elizabeth and I had visited him in Hawick in the Borders

Doulton Fountain, Glasgow.

where his family were originally from. He had been well into his eighties but he was keen to show us around the town, pointing out places of historic interest. In the town square there was a statue of a young lad on a black horse. This was to commemorate the victory of a group of young lads who had kept the English invaders at bay in 1514. Maybe the Scots should have built a wall to keep the English out.

Researching our family history I had discovered that Grandfather's first wife had died from tuberculosis after giving birth to a baby boy in Glasgow in 1900. They had called him Oliver but he didn't survive.

Grandfather must have been devastated. Our grandmother had been his second wife.

"Why were you an only child?" I'd asked Mother.

"My mother had such a traumatic birth having me that George said he wouldn't put her through that again. I don't know how she avoided it," Mother said, "but I know George was very popular with the ladies. I may have brothers and sisters that I don't know about." Looking back, I could have said the same thing.

The bus waited awhile in George Square. Our female tour guide got on board and wished us a good morning. She was very chirpy for so early in the morning. She was going to give a live commentary as the bus toured the city. Other tourists boarded the bus and it soon resembled the United Nations.

The three of us headed for the back seats so we could sit together. What a coincidence - sitting there was a couple from Melbourne.

"Can you tell which part of Australia they're from?" I asked Eileen. "There are no local dialects in Australia," she said. "We don't have a class system." So there are no snobs in Aussie land?

A man took a seat near us, carrying three cameras and smelling of money. "I'm from Texas ma'am," he said.

More tourists got on and soon all the seats were taken. We set off through George Square while our tour guide pointed out places of interest. We saw the Royal Hospital in the distance. It looked grand but foreboding. When I was tracing our family history I found that a young nephew of Granddad's had died there due to a perforated ulcer.

Mother had been taken in there when she was suffering from the same ailment.

"It's a very old hospital," we were told.

"I've heard it's haunted," the Aussie woman said. "Some of the inmates died of fright." Was she kidding?

The bus journeys onwards.

"There's the Bridge of Sighs," we are told. We crane our necks to have a look through the windows. "Don't that sound romantic?" an American woman says. "But why is it called The Bridge of Sighs?"

"It's for the funeral procession," the guide tells us. "The mourners had to cross over the bridge to get to the graveyard. That's why it's called the Bridge of Sighs."

"Oh that aint romantic at all." The American woman says. "It's actually quite depressing."

The bus arrived on Glasgow Green and we saw the Doulton Fountain. It is the largest terracotta fountain in the world and represents the British Empire. There was a statue of Queen Victoria on the top." It was built to commemorate Queen Victoria's Golden Jubilee." Our guide proudly tells us. The fountain is crowded with figurative groups representing Australia, Canada, India and South Africa. The bus stops for a while and we are given historical information about the fountain and also the Peoples Palace that is in the background. We are informed that in bygone days the local women would hang their washing out to dry on the Green. It must have been a sort of communal wash day. I bet they used lots of pegs. This is great though our history lessons were never like this. We peered out through rain soaked windows to have a closer look. I remembered Mother telling me about it. We were sat in her flat in Botanic Road in Liverpool. Over the road was Wavertree Park with its large expanse of grass and its fantastic fountain and botanic gardens. I'd just taken a neighbour's little boy out in his pushchair.

"It's not as nice as the fountain in Albert Park in Middlesbrough," I'd said.

"There's nothing that can compete with the Doulton Fountain in Glasgow," Mother said.

I had asked her if she would like to go back to live in Glasgow. But she just shrugged her shoulders. Maybe she couldn't I thought back then.

Some of the younger passengers got off the bus. It was still raining. We golden oldies remained in our seats. The next attraction was the Riverside Museum. Glasgow has a great maritime history. It was a ship building port and ships regularly sailed down the River Clyde to all over the world. All that was left now of this once thriving industry were the cranes and they may not be there for much longer, we were told. We photographed them from various angles. Cranes don't particularly interest me but these were our link to the past.

Mother and Grandmother had boarded the steamship liner City of Simla. I'd found their details on a passenger list when I was tracing the family history. They'd made the trek down to Liverpool.

They were bound for Calcutta to join Grandfather George who had sailed from Glasgow the previous year. Mother was twelve years of age at the time. Grandfather took up a position as foreman for Bengal Iron and Steel Company in Kulti.

Mother enjoyed living in India. She learned the language and spoke Hindi. The family had a very comfortable life with servants to wait on them.

Although she was away from Scotland for many years, she never lost her Glaswegian accent.

The tour guide said that we would soon see the Clyde Auditorium. The locals called it the Armadillo. Susan Boyle had her audition there for Britain's Got Talent in January 2001, we were informed. I'd watched it on the television. What a voice!

The bus carried on around the city. We came to the University of Glasgow, one of the oldest universities. It has grand Victorian architecture and two spires.

I wondered if Grandfather George studied engineering here when he'd left Hawick and moved to Glasgow? On his marriage certificate it said that he was a journeyman, so he must have served his apprentice as an engineering student.

The bus returned to George Square. There stood a statue of the Duke of Wellington. He was wearing a traffic cone on his head. The tourists were amused and there were lots of suggestions as to why it was put there. It was a good ice breaker though as it got everyone talking. Someone mentions Wellington Boots. "Did he invent Willies," a young Chinese girl asks? Her friend who is sitting next to her whispers in her ear and both girls get a fit of the giggles.

The tour had given us an appetite. We decided to have lunch in Wetherspoons. The building had previously been the old counting house and was owned by the Bank of Scotland.

We went up the steps leading to the grand front entrance. Inside there was an impressive domed ceiling above the wide central bar and the décor was based on the Italian renaissance style. It was enchanting. Pictures and prints of Scottish historical figures adorned the wall. How could anyone have got any counting done in this place? It has too many distractions, me thinks.

CHAPTER 16
Saint Philomenas

We returned from our sightseeing bus tour with a greater knowledge about Glasgow. I had come to the conclusion that as cities go it was up there with the best.

"I have a message for you," Mary the receptionist said. "The priest from Saint Philomena's has rang and he wants you to call him."

I rang the presbytery and the priest answered.

"I have found the baptismal details in our records."

"Wonderful. Can I come and pick it up?"

"Sure, but you will need to be quick as we are setting off for Lourdes this afternoon." I looked at my watch. It was now after two o'clock.

The three of us turned on our heels and set off along Sauchiehall Street. We frantically flagged down the first black taxi cab that came along. "Can you take us to Saint Philomena's?" we shouted at the startled driver. "I thought it was an emergency," he said. "It is as far as I'm concerned."

We didn't know in which area Saint Philomena's was but as the car sped away I realised we were heading for Springburn where Stobhill Hospital was located. So Mother had come back to the area to have Eileen baptised. It made sense if she had intended to have her adopted as it was well away from the address that she had given in the adoption papers. Eileen had been placed in a children's home while the

Interior of Saint Philomena's Church, Glasgow

authorities searched for our mother. But where did Mother go when she left the hospital? I guess that we will never know.

Well, at least Eileen would find out who her godmother was.

We drove along Royston Road looking for number 1255. The driver thought he may have gone past it so he turned the car around and slowly drove back along the road. The church was set away from the road - no wonder we couldn't find it. I was surprised as I was expecting to see a rather dated church but it looked quite modern. We reached the presbytery and rang the door bell. The door was opened by an elderly priest who told us that the parish priest was out. Eileen explained why we were there. He invited us in. "I've found the details of your baptism in our record book. Wait here," he said and went into a sitting room. In the hallway there was a statue of Saint Philomena. It brought back memories. In Middlesbrough we'd had a Saint Philomena's Church. It was about a mile from Nazareth House. On Saturdays the older girls would go there and do some cleaning jobs. One of the chores was to remove the grease from the candlesticks. I didn't mind it at all as it got me out of the home for a day.

Unfortunately, someone in the religious hierarchy decided that there wasn't a Saint Philomena after all and the church had been renamed the Sacred Heart. I did wonder how they would have come to that conclusion. It seemed, thought, that hadn't happened here in Scotland.

The elderly priest returned and handed an envelope to Eileen. "You're fortunate to catch me in, I'm all packed."

We thanked him. Eileen gave him a donation. She opened the envelope. Her Godmother was a Mary Jordan who lived on the Balornack Estate in Springburn. Jordan? Now why did that name ring a bell? There was a Mary Jordan living at the address that Mother had given when she had gone in to Stobhill Hospital to have Eileen. Elizabeth had been given that information when she had searched the electoral role for 1951. When Elizabeth had made enquiries at that address, Mary's daughter didn't know anything about our mother or the baby. But there again she had only been a child herself. Thinking back, I had heard Mother mention that name on the rare occasion that she had talked about her past. I'd wished that I had been more attentive but I was young then and it didn't seem important.

We were walking away from the presbytery when a car drove into the car park. A man got out and opened the boot of the car and took out some golf clubs.

"He must be the parish priest," I said. All the priests that I knew played golf.

I politely wished him a good afternoon and asked if he was the parish priest?

He looked at us suspiciously until Eileen explained why we were here. He was then all smiles. It's that Aussie accent. He said that we could look around the church.

Eileen was delighted.

The priest unlocked the wooden doors. "Let me know when you are leaving," he said.

Eileen and I entered through the side door.

Inside all was quiet, a peaceful haven from the noisy traffic outside. There was a statue of Saint Teresa. On the altar a candle flickered and there was a whiff of incense in the air. It had been a few years since I'd been inside a church. The baptismal font looked dated, it was probably the same one used for Eileen's baptism all those years ago. I sat down on a polished wooden pew.

Our mother had been here and had carried Eileen up this very aisle. So much had happened since then. But we had found her. I said a prayer of thanksgiving. Meanwhile, Eileen was taking plenty of photographs.

Elizabeth doesn't like churches. It's a throwback to Nazareth House. She waited outside for the taxi.

We wondered how Mother could have met this Mary Jordan. They must have been friends for her to be chosen as Eileen's Godmother? More unanswered questions. We could have gone round to the house but Elizabeth had telephoned Mary Jordan's daughter a few years ago. When questioned, she said that she had not heard of our mother or the baby. Thus we decided not to pursue it any further.

We were up early next morning and were once again greeted by a friendly taxi driver. We were catching a train from Queens Street Railway Station and heading back home to Teesside. I was sorry to be leaving as I felt that we could have done the bus tour of the city once again when it was better weather and visited the places of historical interest. I vowed that I would be back one day to visit this fantastic city.

CHAPTER 17
DNA Results

Alan met us at Darlington Railway Station. He was eager to find out about our visit to Scotland.

"Did you find out who your father was then Eileen?"

"No, only that he was a professional businessman," she said. He laughed.

"Your Mother was certainly a woman of mystery," he said. "There's a couple of A4 letters waiting for you and Anne. They must be the results of the DNA tests."

Arriving home I carefully opened the envelope addressed to me. I didn't understand all the jargon but the DNA test had proved that Eileen and I were half siblings on our mother's side. Eileen was reading her letter. It was identical to mine.

"We really do share the same genes pet," I told her. "If you start squinting when you watch the television you've inherited it from our mother."

Since returning from Scotland there was something I was itching to find out.

I logged onto the Find My Past website on my computer and found what I had suspected, details of a marriage that had taken place between Mary Waldie and Hugh Clark. The ceremony had taken place in the Episcopal Church in Glasgow in April 1952, only a few months after Eileen's adoption. So Mother had committed bigamy. The marriage certificate stated that she was a widow but that wasn't true. Raphy was very much alive at that time. It also said that her father George Waldie was deceased but he was living in Glasgow with his third wife. The brazen hussy! I reasoned that because her first marriage to Raphy had taken place in India she probably thought that she could get away with it.

"She should have told us," I said. "We would have been sympathetic knowing the circumstances she was in."

Elizabeth disagreed.

"But how could she? She could have gone to prison."

"If only Raphy would have given her a divorce," I said. "She'd have been free to marry again."

He may have used his Catholicism as a way of getting back at her and not giving her a divorce.

But that was hypocritical when he himself was living with another woman.

Hugh Clark was a good provider - he even sent her money after they were no longer in a relationship. We thought it was because he was generous but he may have just been paying her maintenance.

"Yes, he was just a meal ticket," Alan chipped in. "She didn't like work your Mother. She was used to servants and being waited on hand and foot."

"Yes, but that all stopped when she married Raphy and came to live in Middlesbrough," I said.

Through doing our family history research I was able to trace Raphy's nieces Kathleen and Sheila. Their mother Elizabeth had been Raphy's sister. They told us quite a few things that we didn't know. Apparently Denis would bring Elizabeth and I around to their house. There is a photograph of Denis, Elizabeth and I sitting on a rug in the cousin's garden. They gave me the photograph, which I have included in this book. Their mother had died but Raphy had fallen out with their father and they had lost contact.

Raphy's nieces had also told us that Mother and Raphy came to live with them in their house in Middlesbrough when they returned from India. When Mother changed Denis's nappy she didn't know what to do with it and just flung it in the drawer. She would dress Denis in a brand new outfit every day and would discard the one he had worn the day before. She didn't know any different. Living with Grandfather she had always been well off.

"Well she did give us life and I am grateful to her for that," Eileen said. Elizabeth and I agreed.

CHAPTER 18
Meeting of the Clan

Eileen stayed with us for three weeks. Elizabeth and her family took her on a tour of Middlesbrough and she got to see Nazareth House where Elizabeth and I were brought up by the nuns. And also the Transporter Bridge which I had been on when I had run away from the orphanage all those years ago.

We stayed with my daughter Amanda and her fiancée Richard in Bradford and on a blustery windy day we visited Haworth. The Bronte Parsonage Museum had once been home to the Bronte sisters. Eileen had read their books. She marveled at how tiny the sisters were.

Coming out of the home of the Bronte sisters it was blowing a gale. "It's just like a scene from Wuthering Heights," she laughed. We looked out across the wild moors, bought souvenirs from the little shop attached to the museum and ate lunch in a quaint little tea shop.

The following day we visited the spa town of Ilkley which is twelve miles from Bradford. Eileen loved its Victorian architecture and took plenty of photographs. We enjoyed browsing its gift shops and visited the famous Betty's cafe and tea rooms. We told Eileen to try a fat rascal. She was puzzled. "What is that?" she asked.

"It's a very large fruit scone," I told her. When we showed her one, she told us that in Australia they were known as rock cakes.

Before going back to Australia, Elizabeth and I had arranged to introduce her to other members of our family. I called it the meeting of the clan. It was held in a rather posh restaurant in Leeds. We introduced Eileen to other members of our family, and she discovered that not only was she our sister but she was also an aunt and great aunt. It was lovely for her to chat to her relatives and get to know her blood relations.

We stayed overnight in Bradford with Amanda and Richard and after a hearty breakfast in a cafe in Saltaire we headed north for Newcastle Airport.

On our way to the airport we chatted incessantly. She was leaving with good memories. "Weren't we lucky to have visited Stobhill Hospital," she said, "before they demolished all the buildings. And we got to know something about its history from Michael."

"I know," I said, "and we bombarded him with questions but he didn't seem to mind. I don't think that he will forget us in a hurry," I laughed.

"I got a feel of the place and I imagined Mother walking in there," Eileen said. "I will always have a fondness for the old Stobhill Hospital, the place where I was born. My friends in Australia will laugh when I tell them that I was born in a paupers hospital."

"It's not where you start pet," I told her. "It's where you finish."

"The people are so kind," she said.

"Tom's father-in-law gave us a tour of the Belford when I told him that it was my home when I was a young child. And in Glasgow the priest allowed me to have a look round St Philomena's Church where I was baptized, even giving us the key to the door."

"And you got to know who your Godmother was," I said. "The elusive Mary Jordan."

She nodded.

"And I have walked in Mother's footsteps along the streets of Glasgow. Sauchiehall Street - who could ever forget that name?"

"Well, you are Scottish," I remind her. "You were born in Scotland. 'I belong to Glasgow,'" I sang. She positively beamed.

"At last I have found my roots," she said.

"It's a shame we never found out who your father was though," I said.

"I don't really mind. It's only Mother I was interested in and I feel I've got to know her a little."

"I think fate brought us together," I said. "If Raphy hadn't kept those letters or had died before Mother, we wouldn't be sitting here today. And he died in 1978 - only two years after Mother."

We passed the Angel of The North. Eileen admired it. "Isn't it a wonderful creation?" she said. This time I had my mobile phone ready. She had her camera. "Slow down," I said to Alan, "Eileen and I would like some photos." There

95

wasn't much traffic behind us so we cruised along and managed to take a couple of photographs.

CHAPTER 19
Farewell

We arrived at Newcastle Airport. It was a dull September morning. A large plane was flying above us, its engine roaring. It had just taken off. "Wonder if that's going to Tenerife?" Alan said. "Wish I was on it."

"Alan likes sunnier climates," I explained to Eileen. "I don't mind visiting these places for holidays. But I don't think that I would like to live abroad permanently."

"We are coming into our summer season in Australia," Eileen said. "It can reach 40 degrees."

"Ooh I'm envious," Alan replied.

"You are all very welcome to visit," Eileen said. "I might just take you up on that offer one of these days," Alan said.

We parked and Alan got Eileen's case from the boot of the car. I was feeling sad and thinking that it wasn't too long ago that we had welcomed her here at this airport with open arms and much anticipation. Now, the three weeks had flown by and it had been so nice to have her with us. It was time for her to make the long trek back to Australia. "I'll get a ticket from the car park vending machine," Alan said. Eileen and I headed for the entrance to the airport. She was wheeling her case behind her.

"Bet that is heavier now with all those souvenirs," I said to her. She laughed. "Yes, and I have my black faced sheep to treasure."

The airport was bustling as we went over to the check-in desk but it was too early for her to book in. Alan came over. "It's scandalous the car parking fees," he complained. It was a case of déjà vu. We had at least a two hour wait.

"Might as well have a cuppa," I sighed. "I'm not standing around."

The aroma of coffee and hot snacks was in the air so we followed our noses to the café. Alan went to the counter to order coffee for Eileen and a hot chocolate for me. He joined the long queue.

Elizabeth joined us. She had arrived from Teesside with a friend to say goodbye to Eileen. "Hope it's not too long before we see you again," she said to Eileen. "I feel sad that you are leaving." I agreed.

"Yes, me too. I wish that you didn't live on the other side of the world. But we will definitely keep in touch via email and telephone."

"And Skype," I added. Alan returned with steaming hot drinks and packets of biscuits.

"You are still a vegetarian," Alan said. "Thought we might have tempted you to eat meat again." Eileen smiled.

"I think Eileen would just have thought of those little black faced sheep," I said. "She wouldn't want to eat them."

Soon the time came for Eileen to book in for her flight and not long afterwards it was time to say farewell.

We said our goodbyes and with a heavy heart we waved her off as she went up to the departure lounge. Our lovely, elegant sister. Mother would have been so proud of her.

AFTER THOUGHTS

I have always loved my mother but I didn't know her. I always thought she was very young and couldn't keep me. When I found out I was the youngest, it was just accepted. I can still recall talking to Elizabeth on the phone about everything and then I spoke to Anne and she said- "Is that my little sister?"

These are wonderful memories as to how we first started.

When I learned more about Mary and her life, I saw that it was very difficult for her and I always had compassion for what she went through. It was funny that she was a bigamist. I don't think any of us three thought badly of her.

I must say her children are very understanding and show great sympathy for what her life was like. I have always said Mary was rich and grew less so as the years went by which is extremely hard.

Mary had a very tough time and it was difficult for her to be with a man and love him as best she could when she was so strong willed. I believe she probably would have been a single, independent career woman in today's world.

I can only repeat that I respect my mother and appreciate that she wanted the best for me when she gave me up. I am sure she thought of me over the years and wished to know me as I have always wished to know her.

I am so grateful to Elizabeth and Anne who never gave up trying to find me and that they both went here and there to try and figure out where I was. I love the entire Waldie family and I am so glad I finally know who I am and where I come from. I am very proud to be a Waldie.

All my love

Eileen.

Printed in Great Britain
by Amazon

51879782R00066